DIGIGRAM

Books by Barbara Henning

Poetry

A Day Like Today, 2015
A Swift Passage, 2013
Cities & Memory, 2010
My Autobiography, 2007
Detective Sentences, 2001
Love Makes Thinking Dark, 1995
Smoking in the Twilight Bar, 1988

Fiction

Just Like That, 2018
Thirty Miles to Rosebud, 2009
You, Me and the Insects, 2005
Black Lace, 2001

Editor

Prompt Book: Experiments for Writing Poetry and Fiction, 2020
The Selected Prose of Bobbie Louise Hawkins, 2012
Looking Up Harryette Mullen: Interviews on Sleeping with the Dictionary and Other Works, 2011

DIGIGRAM

Barbara Henning

United Artists Books
New York, 2020

United Artists Books
114 W. 16th Street, 5C
New York, New York 10011

unitedartistsbooks.com
spdbooks.org

for Michah and Linnée

TABLE OF CONTENTS

Raining

—a full moon—wake up late—open my mail—a refund
check—damp and cold—off to the credit union—an
American flag strikes the flag pole—on Avenue B—
an archbishop guides parishioners—catholic-leaning
alternatives—for girl scout cookies—during the crusades—
thousands of children marched to their death—children
crowding—into the earth school—a lanky guy wearing
earmuffs—makes air quotes with his fingers—says
the word "safe"—at 9 pm the storm thins—brownish
fog—the outlook for 2016 somewhat gloomy—German
business leaders urge Russians—uphold a cease-fire—in
the Ukraine—all agree—it's going to stay warm now—
walking home—on Avenue A—a man asks—do you want
cocaine—   *25 Feb 2016*

Kiss Me

—dreaming—on my bike—in Detroit—pull up to a
bungalow—a guy tells me—over there—chain up—I know
him from long ago—inside some kind of sale—models
with skeleton key necklaces—things out of hand—brutal
hand-to-hand—some politicians—outside under an elm
tree—bike gone—sorry they spray it with something—the
lock pops open—bike skeletons everywhere—minus a
wheel or handlebar—under his breath, a curse—he might
shoot me—so cold at the bus stop—I take a cab—passing
the VA hospital—I remember the guy—my hand in his—
he was kissing me—   *26 Feb 2016*

Wham!

—on the lowest speed—up the slight slope—toward the
center of Manhattan—smooth sailing on 6th Ave—raining
and cold—under a plastic poncho—then downhill—
record rain brings wildflowers—in Death Valley—a
NYC policeman forces a man to stand—outside—in his
underwear—in the rain—I can do anything I want, he
says—my dentist likes the bully—you're lucky I don't
vote, he says—about Hitler—well he was listening to the
people, right?—which people? I holler—it's going to come
out—Capote warned People Magazine—with a speed and
power like you've never seen—Wham!—about Hillary—
the dentist hesitates—she's a grandmother—why doesn't
she stay home—with her grandchildren—you must be
kidding—let's talk about the Oscars—some people talk
about Aristotle—while brushing their teeth—please don't
talk—just clean my teeth—Loretta Lynn didn't mean to
knock out her husband's front teeth—click-clack-clack-
clack—be sure to talk—to your physician first—then take
all necessary precautions—   *29 Feb 2016*

3

Siren

—gizmos and widgets—inventors dream of a big hit—I
stand up to read—uh oh this poem was copied—word for
word—from Julie's—irreverent—I can't speak—a little
sting in the air—the party of rich white men—feed off
anxiety of the poor—only five students in class today—
electoral aftermath—immune system shutdown—the
KKK and protestors fight—the length of a city block—in
LA—to be stabbed—by the pole of a confederate flag—on
tv—the bully snorting—with the sound turned off—an
iron stomach is a plus—another bully wants—to be liked
by the alpha bully—awww—definitions unclear and tests
faulty—a siren from my back window—the TV warns rain
and wind—colder weather coming—   *1 Mar 2016*

Morning Glory

—a Ukrainian woman on the bus—asks—how do you
pronounce "via"—Americans have dialects?—she's
excited—and boy does it matter—up the aisle—a
young teenage girl talks into her cell phone—about
"Footlocker"—how they don't have interesting sneakers—
child, she says several times—you're not going to blank
on me, are you?—like a biker child whose been riding all
day—windblown hair—I can't see her face—her sneakers
are turquoise, orange and yellow with green laces and
pink holes—a morning glory is a master of change—in one
day its petals can shift—from blue to pink and sometimes
red—exiting the bus, I glance back—a pudgy 13-year-
old white boy—each number is a child—according to
the American Dialect Society—the word of the year is
"they"—   *2 Mar 2016*

It's Us

—what would you do—I say—in class—to a young
woman—she wants to be a nurse—if a doctor told
you—give this medicine to a patient—you knew he was
wrong—it could be fatal—calm, collected, logical—maybe
you'd lose your job, I say—trying not to panic—the
numbers on the meter jump—she says, calmly—I'd give
it to the patient—we were all like—Whoa!—well, I'd lose
my job—that would be murder—the bully stares back at
us from the mirror—ugly and frightful-haters, bashers,
hucksters—it's us—bundled like an old mummy gliding
down the street—I head toward—a bundle of—yet-to-
bloom crimson peonies—loose ends—catch them up—
quietly with as little movement as possible—   *3 Mar 2016*

So Says Ovid

—Dad died 20 years ago—Jean says—Patti says it, too—
just like that—time sky and night—over and gone—in
the *Times* today—the bully's name appears—above the
fold—eleven times—he-who-must-not-be-named—
laundry in the washer—the dryer—folded into drawers—
vacuum rug—blowing out my bronchi—this and that
horn—order a mattress by hitting a key—sweaters folded
flat—like a sandwich—I say I'm competitive—a young
robust physical therapist laughs—believe oneself well
and one will be well—so says Ovid—at Angelica's eating
chickpeas—Canada and Israel have a robust trade—in
chickpeas—text a question to my ex—where did we buy
those dishes?—ASAP he calls back—his voice so faint—
I can barely hear him—he used to whisper in my ear—
oh I loved him so—my phone line crackly—like an egg
shell inside—

4 Mar 2016

Do Not Come

—fleeing harm—a torrent of human beings—Syria, Iraq,
Afghanistan—warm weather—do not come—near sixty
in New York—Don Yorty points—with his cell phone—an
archive of NYC poets—music blaring—do not come—a
pro-bully rally—warm up the clash—between protestors
and supporters—do not come—"We" have to take a look
at it—do not come—Obama's Hawaiian birth certificate—
the bully says—with more than minimal makeup—and
a bit of eye shadow—do not come—depends upon—
union activist—or reality tv—do not come—the Greece-
Macedonia border—tear gas fired at children—men—
women—do not come—1933—at Mack Ave and Alter
Rd—my ancestors pose—stiff and prepared—for rent—
extra rooms—safety indoors—children fed—2016—
desperate—yet—do not come—do not come—to Europe—
or here—do not come—my right knee stiff—do not
come—stretch it out and in and out—   *8 Mar 2016*

It'll Come to An End

—like Spring out today—don't need a coat—it'll come
to an end—the Maple Leafs coat the islanders—4-3 in a
shootout—the earth moving closer—let the GOP have
the bully—they deserve reality tv—your lungs will be
better now—says the herbalist—try not to think too
much—about politics—the bully whale dying—from
bacteria in his lungs—after killing three young workers—
at Seaworld—this will take a long time—maybe longer
than I have—look at you, Kumar says—drumming the
floor with his foot—you are much much better—at
Trader Joes local organic cukes for 69c—I buy three—
one organ takes over—for another—retired subway cars
dumped into the ocean—now artificial reef—cross-legged
on the floor—Martine and I share Indian food—in the
Steinway building—marble hallways—piano memories—
like misguided golf balls—bouncing 263 yards into a
chilly wind—   *10 Mar 2016*

The Moon

—hang a dress—in the lobby—wrong size—for 2016—
once twirled around—like a flower—on a highway—
soon on a hanger—in some other closet—reading Walter
Benjamin—*Berlin Childhood*—what was and what might
be—a shelter—the rhythm of the railway—ringing of a
bell—a butterfly hovering—each passing moment—to
gaze—to touch—as a child—the moon—out a Berlin
window—*High above the horizon*—then a pale circle—in the
afternoon sky—growing growing growing—until it sucks
up—tears apart—people place—iron rails—like Krishna
opening the veil—*it was my farewell*—Benjamin writes—*"O
star and flower, spirit and dress, love, grief, time and eternity!"*—
In 1938—this miniature deleted—perhaps, too much—the
melancholic grip—start over—at the beginning—with
children—the weight of the book—pressing against my
chest—drift off—*I collected what I wanted to take across*—he
writes—from then to now—   *13 Mar 2016*

Ethics

—damp, cold, windy—in a single fluid motion—the player
shoves—his mouthpiece into position—soars across the
court—rain will continue—emissions, too—in the next
century—the shoreline will rise—three feet—then it'll dry
a bit—I head north—Lafayette becoming Park—be careful
what you say—to Siri—I wanna jump off a bridge—she
might give directions—a woman with Zika—the fetus
may or may not—14,000 Syrian migrants—in desperate
condition—hepatitis A—a quarter-million children—
some eat animal feed and grass—a school teacher says—
with an ethic of self interest—no more taxes or social
programs—lucky for a public sector job—before he got
big—tyrannosaurus got smart—tadpoles in outer space
survive—but come home with two heads—   *14 Mar 2016*

You Knew Before

—to follow the circle—around the park—a big hawk nest—
mother gingko—look away—playground and basketball—
melancholic clouds—if he gets his way—Hillary says—it'll
be bully Christmas in the Kremlin—just an excuse—to
hawk steaks and wine—one hundred sheep—huddle in
a circle—under a blue light—low and breathy—Daymé
Arocena sings—*you knew before—you knew before—what
could have been*—Avenue A to 7th Street—stand still—one
hand over the other—over your heart—in Brussels—more
than thirty pounds—of explosives—over the East River, a
full moon—   *21 Mar 2016*

Safety

—on the ground—a clutter of acorns—"Look," the
boy says on the tv—"Real water!"—with an air—
of nonchalance—the woman flicks ashes—from a
cigarette—the dictator waves his hand—*never would
I—tarnish—my own name*—a volcano erupts—a cloud of
ash—seven miles skyward—a suitcase full of nails and
bolts—wildfires—in Kansas—the sturdy old home—piles
of bricks and ash—a locket—between a woman's face—
and a toddler's—Allen's ashes—won't stay put—some
on the table—my fingers grainy—with his body—how to
maximize—our assets—off with our shoes—back pocket
cocaine—breathless—up we go—on a downward-moving
escalator—safe at last—   *29 Mar 2016*

A Flower, An Olive, An Idea

—out the back window—a flowering pear—little white
buds—each morning—9.5 million people—turn on their
showers—I pack away—winter coat and boots—flip open
the blinds—across the yard—in a rear window—a man
shaving—off to meet—Dennis and Phyllis—at Mogador—
on the sidewalk—a nearly nude woman—with a giant
purple bouffant—Benjamin Franklin used to—stand
naked in front of—his window—to be in love—with a
flower, an olive, an idea—at night—a cold-air bath—
thunder—the sound of rain on pavement—turn off the
lights—lie in bed—in the dark—and listen—my arms
crossed—over my bare chest—the child I was—am now—
Mama and Daddy—I say out loud—   *2 Apr 2016*

Walled-In

—along the Hudson river—children—on a merry go
round—screaming and peddling—swivels and swoops—
not quite enough rain—CNN will stream—the so-called
debate—a new digital device—a rapid stream of single
words—one after the other—a red ferry glides back and
forth—yellow cabs now and then—just past noon, the
sun, a woman—in a brown coat strolling along—with
notebook—stops, looks—under black sunglasses—jots
down something—perhaps a poet—or a journalist—in
Arizona—or Michigan or Long Island—at a bully rally—
Look dad!—says the little boy—snipers!—our American
dream—a walled-in community—with smaller walled-in
homes—as the jagged hills and walls—recede into the
distance—in Battery Park—a little girl swings—back and
forth—scooping up the air—   *23 Apr 2016*

River God

—in black and white—outside the Art Institute—1984—
my two children—on the belly of a river god—once
lying—beside the Garonne in France—bare-chested—
looking over a baby angel—then over—the ruins of
Detroit—our birth city—your time will come, he says—
Néné's seven-year-old smile—fine hair in the wind—
Mook squinting—a few months later—I-80 to New York
City—behind us Zug Island—and the charred remains—in
Narcisse—75,000 snakes—awaken—from an eight-month
nap—tumble over a craggy landscape—tangled knots—a
single aim—reproduction—how I miss—my children as
children—today's light over the shrubs—a small plane
coasting—through the sky—rush into the car—cry over a
scrape—a little league baseball game—be quiet—the boys
reclining—beside my grown daughter—watching tv—their
feet overlapping— *6 May 2016*

To Get By

—the inmate—picked up—in the woods—off the Garden
State—a week on the run—70 something—too warm—
traffic dense—biking in a cloud of smoke—yell at ubers—
big black cars—the air thick—sitting in the park—a
man—with big black boots—white wrinkled pants—
trouble walking—lifting his knees—one at a time—as if
with a pulley—3 hours sleep last night—must drive a cab
12 hours—to get by—you're killing yourself—with eyes
closed—at St Marks—the podium poet—whisks it up—
stiff peaks form—Don Yorty takes a swig—of vodka—
then the chatty—New York school—backwards—and
sideways—out the door—we go—at 2nd Ave and 10th
Street—
9 May 2016

Stumble

—Alter Rd near the Detroit River—naked, holding a
kitchen towel—over my crotch—the chubby new wife—
in an apron—shocked—when oxygen is low—naked
mole rats—flip a switch to survive—metabolic—Tunick
shoots—a large group of naked people—no surprise—no
news—now it's her dream—I try to apologize—for my
body parts—but she's cooking—a one man militia—rushes
through the hallway—angry—skedaddle out of there—
just in time—to stumble down the aisle—he's holding—
something yellow—a flower—wake up—to news—a
bombed hospital—in Afghanistan—a doctor—one leg torn
off—talks into a cell phone—good-bye—dear wife—please
take care—of the children—   *15 May 2016*

We Can, We Can

—truth and lies viral—rampant hatred—an American
man dumps—boiling water—on two sleeping men—a
curfew to quell rioting—after a police shooting—if only—
as simple as—a belief—in ancestors—in Madagascar—
wearing red—at the waterfront—may incite—an
ancestor's wrath—naked under a sheet at 1 a.m.—in
the U.P.—the night so quiet—the trees still—a slight
ringing—in the mind—we *can* squash Mr. Bully—we can
we can—dear mother—dear grandmother—please—send
qi—outside a high pitched ringing—between the rising
wind—and a chorus of crickets—all other animals—in
this house—are sound asleep—   *1 Aug 2016*

Let Me Know

—the sun's hot—a cool breeze—off Lake Superior—a
path along the shore—peddling behind a woman—on
a turquoise upright bike—a polluted sky—does not
have—the advantage—of producing—these atmospheric
colors—sunflowers follow—the rising sun—up, over and
westward—as I pass the woman on the bike—I say—"I'm
going slightly faster than you, dear"—by law many
mothers—are unable to pass on—their citizenship to their
children—but for fathers—a different story—when a pass
is made—four defenders charge—from the net—trying
to block—the oncoming shot—a year later—a committee
of American men—will meet to decide—the rights of
women—the woman on the turquoise bike laughs—
"Thanks," she says, "for letting me know"—   *4 Aug 2016*

A Misstep, a Slip

—in the middle—of the road—a baby doe—then
another—then a mother—all three standing still—turn
and slip back—into the forest—American Pharoah—
earned the right—to spend old age in a barn—a misstep,
a slip—could have been death—my sister turns the car
left—a clearing and a two story house—three dogs out
the door—Baily circles us—madly barking and licking—
in the house—the other woman—glides across the
floor—in a flowery house dress—like a soft tent—with
long kinky yellow hair—"I can see the resemblance"—
eyebrows lift, a shrug—outside in the shade—my sister's
flower gardens—overgrown—somewhere, someplace—
we buried most of Allen's ashes—then the storm took
the bridge—the river branched—down in the bottom of
my bag—a silver capsule—"couldn't leave him—with a
subletter"—   *5 Aug 2016*

We Branch Out

for Barbara Spires

—Amish—we were Mennonite—and French Canadian
Catholic—nine to ten—in every family—pregnant
women—easy to dominate—horizontally and vertically—
we branch out—all related—tree trunks shatter—branches
clutter—in the storm—on a boat from Europe—some
Nelly loses her children and husband—remarries—more
children—works in a paper mill—her husband a fruit
vender—when adversity hits—the birds chirp, squawk,
tweet—their syrinx branching—into left and right
lungs—in coal country—black lung disease—waiting
for the Mennonites—with their vans and hammers—
godmother, namesake—after the fire—your baby dies—
you pack up and move—far away—another child, divorce,
remarriage—men don't do well alone—so they say—you
liked casinos—now in Resthaven Memorial Park—
Shawnee, Pottawtomie County—far from the coast—and
Hurricane Matthew—where the waters rise waist-high—
or the Seine—where Daubigny once converted a boat—
into a floating studio—   *17 Oct 2016*

Under Arrest

—on 38th St—Dr. Wallstein unplugs my ear—then 52nd
Street—Nancy unplugs my brain—if we unplug the
rivers—fish will return—unplugged—the bully stalks
Hillary—across the stage—you stuck your tongue in my
mouth—a journalist accuses—he promises steak at Pete
Luger's—even in a very tiny space—you can create a
nuisance—with .3% increase in social security—millions
of unpaid bills—with four tiny flakes of donut glaze—
today—you are under arrest—for crystal meth—and for
watching a city burn—outside your window—while the
bandit munches—on pignoli cookies—or a 1,910 pound
pumpkin—grown by his third grade teacher— *19 Oct 2016*

On Air, On Land, At Sea

—when surfing in 28 degree water—or stuck in traffic—
for 63 hours a year—your brain freezes—your chin
gets stiff—no angry mobs in Tehran—shouting "Death
to America"—No McDonald's in Tehran—instead, a
homegrown Mash Donald—dreaming—of a woman
with blonde hair—chin length—at a restaurant table—
with a younger dejected bully—hey, don't worry—she
says looking down at him—I'll let you see *em* later—he
drops his head—a sad puppy—so sad—so horrible—
when the phone rings—we all wake up—to headlines
with his name—oh no—and they're just not true—he
says—everyone must love me—digital twitter talk—
can't be recaptured—and you can't bury it—it's out
there—scattered in air, on land, at sea—North Africa to
Europe—Seawatch reports—2400 migrants rescued—
four children dead—   *26 Oct 2016*

Swiped

—on the subway—a tall young man stands over me—
baseball hat—headphones—fine curved upper arms—
his head grazes the ceiling—bending the cost curve—
essential for long term well-being—the train leans
left—a woman leans over—to adjust the strap—on one
of her heels—perhaps—the possibility of coupling—
swiped away—early on—headphones can be worn—as
a necklace—with only a hint of a head and tail—the
common swift—curves its wings—staying in the air—for
ten months—this or that haircut—and bang—you're an
old man—don't even think—about a tank top—a kind
of mental framework—takes hold—I'm worried—about
a friend—her hands shaking—her muscles rigid—even
though—it's cold and rainy—I wear a skirt—the young
man wears a tee-shirt—and Glen Close—tones her
bones and sinews—on Sunset Boulevard—let's all just
pretend—it's warm outside—   *27 Oct 2016*

Judge Judy

—in the morning—it's raining—yellow locust leaves—
on the cement—people silent, stooped over—difficult
to explain—the outcome—to the children—in yoga
class—we are crying—can't fathom—how anyone could
listen—and still vote—for the bully—and his macho
pigs—widespread reports of fires—broken windows—
ten percent of college grads—believe Judge Judy—is
a Supreme Court Justice—and they hate Hillary—
Europeans have women leaders—and social-welfare—we
have a commander in chief—and a military industrial
complex—as first lady—they once spit on her—thousands
of dead pigs—floating down a river in China—they called
her a dirty socialist—the thing is—they *need*—universal
health care—they need—universal *mental* care—in Union
Square—thousands and thousands—of pastel post-it
notes—growing—a wall of mourning—   *9 Nov 2016*

You Want It Darker

—on a park bench—downtown Pensacola—a guy with
white hair and beard—strums a guitar—baseball cap—
they used to—hang people in this park—a tiny ant—visits
a brown leaf—on the sidewalk—another guy—sticks out
his tongue—comes closer—sticks his tongue out again—
some men never disclose—their true ailments—are you
dissing me, I ask—*I don't know that word*—a New York
City word—*I'm from Belfast, Ireland—born 1958*—skinny
legs, knee length pants—how'd you get—that black
eye?—*Deborah did it—in the bar—last night—kaboom—I
got woman problems*—he smiles—two yellow teeth—
alcohol problems?—*and weed and everything—what's your
name, darling?*—Barbara—*I'm Pete*—he reaches—for my
hand—a Muslim college student—refuses to shake the
hand—of her bully-supporting roommate—the night
after—the silent majority—she says—speckled the
streets—sporting red caps—like military uniforms—Pete's
a poet—off to a reading—the Knicks are far from—
high playoff peaks—after election day we're far off,
too—losing Leonard Cohen—you want it darker—he
sings—you get it darker—democracy's *not* coming—to the
USA—anytime soon—when I pass—the guitarist—a gulf
wind clanks—the flag's cord—against the pole—and his
hat reads—"I'm happy"—   *13 Nov 2016*

27

Ahimsa

—she works for Hillary—her twin, a doctor—raised
orthodox—likes the bully—less taxes, no Obamacare—
doesn't like Muslims—Hitler no matter—Baptists in
Alabama—hold a mock baptism—forgive all his sins—
some would prefer—a baptism of fire—the lacking
silent majority—long islanders—michiganders—with
home, car, pension, swimming pool—a decent job—in
tool and die—or the fire department—big house—
board of education—administration—*what do minorities
have on you*—I don't like Hillary—can't say why—just
don't—he doesn't really mean—what he says—after
all—the president can't do anything—anyhow—ha ha
ha—an unfiltered text box—loose cannon—twisted
rhetoric—it's because she's a woman—a friend says—
but what about Sarah Palin—an angry woman—on the
bus says—he's so attractive—!#@!?—*Ahimsa.* I say to
myself, *ahimsa*—   *14 Nov 2016*

Coprolalia

—early morning—fall into a dream—dragonflies buzz
around me—and Paul Ryan—smiles—with his widow's
peak—like Dracula—saying—we're going to privatize—
all the prisons—then my sister lends my car—to a guy
I'm seeing—you don't know him—I yell—you should ask
first—fucking asshole—now she's asleep—on the sofa—I
feel guilty—for swearing at her—but I do it again—
coprolalia—compulsive swearing—can't help it—fuck
it—at dawn—downtown Detroit—fuck it—it's still dark—
and I'm still dreaming—Eric Clapton said—he would
stop touring—I swear—this is it—no more—then I start
running—into a dangerous-at-night-neighborhood—I
see the house—where Linnée was born—someone else
lives there—all the neighbors gone—curling up—in a
corner—of the porch—waiting for daylight—so the hoods
won't see me—before that—making sweet love—with
that guy—who's now driving my car—down Trumbull
Avenue—heading for I94—   *25 Nov 2016*

The Funky Chicken

—wake up—creaky, old—falling apart—when the
winds—from the south—hit the mountains—mid
country—smoke and ash—obscure the night sky—to
chase away misfortune—Amazonian shamans light a
stick—of palo santo—to chase away misfortune—say
"no" "not that"—say it loudly—like Mr. Blow—peddle
onward—to yoga—in a purple coat, red plaid scarf, green
hat, grey pants, blue-green-black striped socks—colors
roll with the wind—wheels pass over—unsuspecting
insects—at Bowery and First—chain up—ring bell—do
the funky chicken—preen—scratch head—march in
unison—poke a wing—here and there—then forward
and up—with your tail—then flip flap your wings—
homeward, the cement covered—in golden leaves—the
air crisp—chain up—on the corner—two men—deeply
inhaling—I cover my mouth and nose—with a scarf—
give a five to the bodega clerk—passing the smokers
again—carrying home my daily addiction—two packs
of—chocolate peanut butter cups—   *27 Nov 2016*

On the Q

—to Manhattan—through the slit—between my eyelids—
an almost empty car—two women dozing—one leans
forward—hair cropped—ear level—mid sixties—freckles—
arms crossed—head bobbing—as the train jerks—"little
brown bag"—on her lap—the other woman—one leg
crossed—over the other—shoulder length—glistening
black hair—leaning to the side—head against rail—
dozing—trading relatively quiet today—investors
returning—from Thanksgiving vacation—the car quiet—
climbs over—the Manhattan bridge—behind the ropes
and rails—the Brooklyn Bridge—dark scattered clouds—
the western sun—a golden hue—a six foot three inch—
Justinian cross—over the World Trade Center—young
adults—brought here as children—soon sent—to places
they never knew—underground we go—the conductor
says—this is Canal Street—Chinatown—the older
woman—stands up—head still bowed—doors open—and
then she's gone—   *28 Nov 2016*

No Matter What

—a brown oak leaf falls—on the windshield—of the
M14 bus—catches in the corner—a woman—in a grey
felt hat—leans against me—a Milwaukee man says he
felt cornered—between two unlikeable options—when
a monkey loses status—his immune system weakens—
mortgage rates climb—ordinary people—pause to
consider—house ownership—the elephant pivots—
towards the donkey—around the corner we go—stocks
in rally mode—wheels passing over—tangled ideology—
more about psychology—the hormones in his brain—
not there anymore—the NYC mayor says—no matter—
what—the bully does—we ain't changing—rising sea
levels—not an abstract concept—as the season shifts—so
do our molecules—it's damp today—but unseasonably
warm—the ice cap melting—soon Cassini will—shift
orbit—sneaking closer—and closer—on September 15—at
8:07 am—crashing into Saturn—we're all a little on edge
now—waiting to see—what'll happen next—   *29 Nov 2016*

String Ball

for Nevine Michaan and Charles Blow

*—the body's organized—on a square—*so says Yogi Nevine—
I walk around Tompkins Square—all four corners—surely
this is the center—of the universe—*the goal in life—*
*should be joy—*in Larung Gar—the Chinese—are tearing
apart—Tibetan monastic dwellings—*plan your life—like*
a chess game—move analytically—with intent—it's very
*practical—the way to attain joy—*even for civilians—trapped
in Aleppo—with artillery shelling overhead—*defeat in*
*life—is bitterness—*buck up—writes Charles Blow—it's
over—the bully's—in the white house—for the time
being—alt-right is not—a computer command—they're
a batch of fanatical racists—*if you're happy—you'll help*
*everyone—if you're miserable—you won't help anyone—*in
Shuafat—a refugee camp—in Jerusalem—Baha helps
the orphans—work, find direction, survive—then a
drive-by—ten bullets—one of the children—will surely—
take his place—you can follow—fake news sites—from
one to another—unravel the molecular structure—
of ribosomes—a tangled mess of rubber bands—and
coiled wires—a new pattern—of income equality—life
expectancy in the US—declines slightly—*be careful—*
it's like a string ball—if we keep going around—in the same
direction—we will surely unravel—   1 Dec 2016

33

Slow Snow

—on Sunday night—do the dishes—take a hot
bath—watch an abandoned boat—on tv—cross the
Mediterranean—crammed full—of migrants—watch
it capsize—the planet's hotter—this year—old racial
hatreds—floating on a platform—beside melting glaciers—
Mr. Einaudi plays piano—I calm myself—by reading
Sebald—some dreamy place—between living and dying—
walk along the park—scarf, hat, little flats—slow snow
melting—on my shoulders—young people—smoking—
between one bar and another—I was once young, too—
walked this same block—on 7th Street—from Avenue A to
B—waiting for Michael in the Horseshoe Bar— *30 Dec 2016*

Common Thought

—Queen Elizabeth to her guard—that's quite all right—
next time I'll ring beforehand—so you don't have—to
shoot me—in Cucina de Pese—reach into my bag for my
cell—shoot—left it home—pick up a flier—write on the
back—pen sliding over paper—January 4, 1960—my
mother's death date—a voice from another table—*when
mother died—I was 14 and my brother was nine—even though
we were in prep school—I looked after him*—for our family—
public school—tastee bread and bean sandwiches—we
took care—of each other—I was the oldest—56 years
later—to woo voters—a gospel concert in Richmond—
sponsored by the Koch brothers—hurray for the oil
industry—when they pay—some of us sing—while others
cry—I put my face in my hands—contrary to common
thought—family isn't—everything—   *4 Jan 2017*

Slow Down

—with Parkinson's—my friend—doesn't qualify—for
disability—so says the voice—at Social Security—her
mistake—last year—making more than a thousand a
month—even with rent low for NYC—impossible—driving
a cab—12 hours a day—shaky hands—stiff slow down—in
Cleveland—old men—shake their fists—at holes in the
sky—where steel mills—used to be—from circular—to
rectilinear—blue jays drive—hawks and owls—from their
territories—"Everyone's trying—to push me—do this—do
that—why is this happening?"—losing focus—gonna buy
vitamins—from a man she knows—puts her head down—
on the table—the poet—weeps and sings—merciless
bureaucracies—merciless sky—and I wonder—who is the
hawk—where is the owl—   *5 Jan 2017*

I Love Yoga

*—I love yoga—I'm only having the cleaning woman—once a week now—next month we're going to the Canary Islands—*the heights of—trendy exercise—a careful moon watcher notes—from 127 million miles away—we sit down—for dinner—at Angelica's Kitchen—our favorite table—Lewis says he'll retire—in a few years—Harris going to Mexico—can't afford rent here—snow covers the streets and cars—the trees in the park—branches crisscrossing overhead—snow in Istanbul today, too—magical—standing in front of—Cafe Pick Me Up—now empty—from $6,000 a month to $15,000—soon to be Starbucks—snow on my shoulders—behind a cloud—a super moon—seven percent larger than normal—step carefully—an icy sidewalk—Avenue A—one empty building—after another—luxury apartments for rent—   *7 Jan 2017*

Prediction

—temp up twenty degrees—Nasdaq Biotec up 8 percent—
unseasonably warm—an unscheduled bus—hold my
hands in prayer—he reopens!—zoom no traffic—Union
Square Station—escalator broken—a woman with baby
buggy—standing at the stairs—out of breath—a young
man on cell phone—sagging pants—could you help
her?—he looks at me—with hatred—then at her—she's
black—ok—he takes her stroller down—looking back—
over his shoulder—snarls at me—third person subjective—
the way—we are held—accountable—for past—acts of
violence—the result—of unbearable loss—why then—this
belief—in possibility—a man begging—I pass a dollar—as
if something—in the morning—they predict—the mercury
will plummet—   *12 Jan 2017*

Mid-Jump

—frozen snow—on sidewalk, cars, trees—in the *Times* a
photo of frolicking fish—frozen in a wall of water—mid-
jump—time to hibernate—bundle up—Mama called me
dear—she called Dad, *honey*—our dear leader promised
everyone health coverage—ha ha!—refracting bullets—
detour in the 40th precinct—erratic—bounce—hey
sweetie—where you going, *honey bunch?*—Do you have an
internet connection—you may be able to stream this—
adding another layer—to the already edgy sentiment—in
DC never-ending sirens—reds, light greens, blues—Elsa
the baroness skips along—a stream of edgy one word
lines—one sound—telegrams to the world—   *19 Jan 2017*

The Night Before

—a man in the airport—kicks a woman—wearing a head
scarf—across from Rikers—tourists on a safari—take
photos—of a coyote with eight pups—you're working
too hard—I say—to the man—in Superior Burger—he's
edgy—how it is—working as a clerk—at a lunch counter—
in carnivals—lemonade stand—a photo booth—drove an
ice cream truck—ran a contentious English department—
nothing quite as dramatic—however—as Clare
Hollingworth—a war correspondent—in 1939—alone in
a car—between Poland and Germany—the wind lifted—
the tarpaulin—and she saw—what was to come—at 80
shinnying up a lamppost—in Tiananmen Square—dying at
105—an incredible life—kudos to Ms. Hollingworth—I jog
around the square—trees bare—twigs brittle—on Avenue
A—just a whiff of smoke—coughing—then onward
toward 1st Ave—for apples and oranges—   *20 Jan 2017*

Flip It

—gusts of wind and pigeon feathers—blowing east and
north—biking west and south—to the drug store on 2nd
Ave—run into Elinor—a facebook group—downtown
women fighting the bully—flip it in 2018—coughing
on 1st Ave—pull over—adjust to less oxygen—adjust to
unprecedented assaults—on what is and is not—passing
through the park—nearly every president—has a learning
curve—but this one is exceptional—yes, sir—Mexico *is*
our next door *neighbor*—follow the curves around the
benches—the large oak and elm trees—like skeletons
passing through—like coming home—just glide in, around
and out the side gate—overhead a squirrel's nest—with an
outer skeleton of twigs—see someone I used to know—
wave—zoom by—on 7th Street in front of my building—
take off helmet, glasses and lock up bike—open the door
for a neighbor—carrying a big bag—I like your haircut,
she says—Philip Glass is happy—when someone says—*It
doesn't sound like you*—   *27 Jan 2017*

So Do I

—hey buddy—are you looking for a glove?—the bank,
the hardware store, the health food store—apples $3.80
a pound—that's crazy—turn the corner—Ave A to 7th
Street—surprise—my-ex on the sidewalk—when I was in
the dentist's chair—I imagined you kissing me—wanna sit
in the park?—let's go to your place—for a minute—look
around—the first one to leap up—a standing ovation—not
that, back off—sit down—can you at least hug me?—best
to stay here and there—I signal the space—between us—
he nods—the Atlas 5 rocket lifts off at 9:45—roars into a
clear sky—I look for you everywhere—so do I—why did
you get married?—he shrugs—the sheer physical toil—
required to survive—without electricity—we might have
gone on—slightly hungry—you wanted *that* life—he nods
again—then I say I love you—he says, I love you too—
then he's gone—just like that—   *24 Feb 2017*

Come Here

—with tiny hands—and a tiny brain—like the
tyrannosaurs—ha ha—the bully had to develop
something—an ability to lie and deny—even when myths
are dispelled—their effects linger—it's possible to hack
into a phone—or a car—with only sound waves—tiny
accelerometers—under the scholar's trees—open an
envelope—rent increase $200.00—google mania—first
floor, no fee, rent stabilized—Brooklyn studio—quiet,
tree-lined—but I like living here—come on, Barbara—
says the landlord—when you get older, you *should*
move—we will *never*—give you—a rent stabilized
apartment—a commodity—a troublemaker brainiac—
Tony Conrad—crooks his finger—come here—I'm gonna
wreck your brain—a crack—in the cave—with ulnar
nerve repaired—DeGrom's back on the mound—at 97
miles per hour—   *20 Mar 2017*

Woman With A Cane

—Second Avenue bus stop—at 50th Street—woman with
a cane—points at a building—across the way—"A lift
once fell—from that building—and killed a pedestrian"—
another woman—tall under a big straw hat—says—
"My name's on a list—for an apartment there"—in
Brownsville, Texas—trucks with loudspeakers—move
slowly—through cane fields—"Anyone hiding—get out
now—before the burn—no one will arrest you—just
get out"—the tall woman—in a long coat—much too
warm—for today—carries a black biker's bag—bright red
lipstick—rouge on her cheeks—I find a seat—beside a
hunched over woman—messy uncombed blond hair—she
laughs—nudges me with her elbow—like a female glass
frog—sitting on her eggs—nudge her—but she won't
budge—loudly, she says—"Look at her makeup! Ha ha"—
looking at me—then she says it—again and again—"Leave
her alone"—I whisper—day long humidity—grey skies—a
renovated public bathroom—under stately London plane
trees—pull the rope to signal stop—the woman in the hat
stands up, too—stately posture—tall in her tattered coat—
"Look at her makeup! Ha ha"—outside at 14th street—a
whiff of something long gone—   *29 Mar 2017*

From Every Angle

—melted sand—then sheets float—in molten tin—
silvered—a mirror image—nervous—elbow tweaked—loss
tingling—through out—away I go—on Easter Sunday—by
car and truck—goodbye—dear elms and scholar trees—
Mourad—Mogador—Commodities—Veselka—Sally—
Sylvia—Yoga East—Katonah—Essex Stationary—Genny—
Cliff—The Poetry Project—my neighbors—life on 7th
Street—you're not moving—are you?—pushed—into the
subway—into the boroughs—think the opposite—that
great yoga sutra—tonight—I'll be sleeping—in the same
bed—yes?—from every angle—exactly the same—my
body, my books—on 12th Street—in Brooklyn—head
pointing south—as usual—sound asleep—under the same
sheets and blankets—   *16 Apr 2017*

Phantom of the North

—a great grey owl—on a tree top—suddenly drops
down—slyly hooks—a tiny creature—hiding—in a
tunnel of snow—two feet deep—the bully's education
czar—signs her ok—on predatory 16 percent fees—
for defaulted student loans—buried in the details—
an administrative tweak—garnished social security
checks—old age despair—for the Roman's—an owl's
hoot—a forecast of imminent death—two great horned
owls—spotted today—in Prospect Park—*whistle   bark
shriek   scream   hoot*—for the bully, for his czar—*whistle
bark   shriek   scream   hoot*—stick a pin in a doll—
damn—a twinge in my right elbow—dismantling and
reassembling—boxes of books—the old man—in the
Szechwan restaurant—writes down #15—brings a #13—
his daughter and son—scold him in Chinese—no snow
today—albeit a cold April day—   *18 Apr 2017*

It All Depends

—upon a wizened old woman—missing two front
teeth—an old skull cap—big men's levis—full of holes—a
shopping cart—no tax loopholes—she scowls at me,
then apologizes—trains seem safer than the 80s—I
say—*depends on who you are—and where you are*—true,
true—so many changes—the crowded car listens—when
I stand up—she stretches out her hand—*I'm Bernice
and I'm 62*—I'm Barbara, 68—and I wonder—about
her childhood—and then what?—if I have golfer's
elbow—medicare covers physical therapy—but the $20
co-pay—for some—a snorkel extends and bends like an
elbow—with a pointer finger—the gardener in Tompkins
Square—pokes a small hole into the soil—I pick up my
mail—at 144 7th Street—put keys on the counter—tear
my name off the mailbox—no nostalgia allowed—F train
home—nine stops—trees along 12th street in Brooklyn—
light green, locust, elm, poplar, locust, gingko, maple, and
two I don't yet know—   *27 Apr 2017*

Spilling Over

—on Houston—a garden—with young people—smoking
and napping—an ex-coal worker—can't breathe—
wants his job back—coal ash arsenic mercury lead—in
landfills and bodies of water—between Saturn and its
innermost ring—the patter of a summer squall—then a
drifting tone—in the branches—of a giant elm—the baby
and me—fade into flickering leaves—into a Himalyan
crevasse—a rock climber falls—we keep climbing—
downward—into the subway station—a young woman—
with two little ones in tow—talking on her cell—to hold a
fossil—to clutch a fragment—thirty-five years—standing—
in this same spot—with Né and Mook—it's raining
today—and the baby is a man now—he drills a hole—in
the ceiling—of my new apartment—for a plant—the
leaves spilling over the pot—   *28 Apr 2017*

A Form of Light

—on the F train—I imagine—cutting a woman's hair—
revealing her face—reaching—into her bag—she takes
out—a small bottle of brandy—takes a swig—less is
not more—more is more—the oceans littered—with
trillions—of tiny plastic particles—here and there—a red-
flag warning—weighed—measured—the object—of their
attention—poked   scanned   xray'd—the NFL won't
buy—a pig in a poke—at St Marks—Laurie Anderson
tells—a story—with her violin—staying with an Amish
couple—and a grandmother—who coerces—a little
boy—into kissing her—when he doesn't want to—a first
lesson—Anderson says—in sex without—affection—the
violin tips—turns—when a mushroom glows—energy
is released—in the form of light—for ten minutes—then
whoosh—gone—low-key—skullcap—no makeup—love
her—and her violin—   *29 Apr 2017*

Blink

—on the F train—I'm reading the *Times*—on my cell—a
pink protestor—laughs—at the bully's white man—an
outright lie—hand-cuffed—for election disruption—the
Ayatollah—vows a slap in the face—when the bully
blinks—you-may-or-may-not—miss it—an old man—in
denim overhauls—stares out the window—inside the
tunnel—hundreds scrolling—Kerouac's typed 120-foot
paper roll—now in a museum—a guy with a kindle—in
front of his face—Derek Jeter's face—now on a plaque—in
the Bronx—Putin's opposition—a splash of chemicals—
now blind—Dr Kavner says—world wide problem—not
blinking—staring into screens—spring models—with
smudged eye make up—fashionable black rings—
one pink-lipped girl—rests her face—on her friend's
shoulder—a guy passes through the car—do rag, sleeveless
shirt—a teen wearing pink lipstick—opens a package—of
multicolored socks—neon green, pink, blue—and the train
c-r-a-w-l-s toward Manhattan—   *10 May 2017*

50

How Are You?

—I80 in Pennsylvania—feathers flying—from a truck—my
phone rings—your former—domestic partner—a dream—
he had about me—how are you—feathers continue—to
fly here and there—natural selection—sometimes loses
control—could be—the consequence—of sexual desire—
your home phone changed—and my wife—deleted
all your texts—banned from flying—overhead—with
a plum skirt—covered in black feathers—I speed up—
well nothing's here—one way or the other—fill-in-
the-blank—I accelerate—pass the truck—small cages—
crammed with live chickens—necks and legs—bound
tightly—together—they can't move—feet sticking out of
openings—in cages—feathers everywhere—the speed you
throw—the ball—affects the curve—on the way—around
the mountain—with glassy eyes—as if impossible—to
acknowledge—our shared mortality—   *11 May 2017*

Gently, So Gently

—to avoid the draft—at nineteen—Allen marries—and
divorces—he doesn't tell me—after he dies—an email—
from his ex—a funky trailer—in Abiquiu—two cats, a
dog—white sand, red rocks—in a cafe we talk—a young
couple in a photo—dreamy as in a dream—where the
bully's selling—*all* our things—books and photos—even
my clothing—to a library—like a dog—following a
scent—a counter attack—cyber blurring—on a shelf—an
old coat with holes—no buttons—the Roman streets—full
of holes—is anybody looking?—gently, so gently—put on
the coat—in its place—leave behind—a delicate—white
bridal dress—with a note—dear funky—we too—used to
love—a bit of lace—   *12 May 2017*

As the Bully World Turns

—on the White House flagpole—an eagle—when
vervet monkeys—see a marital eagle—they make a low
pitched—staccato *r-r-raup*—then run for the suburbs—at
the fraternal order—as the bully world turns—old men
pose—hands against the wall—in cowboy hats—an icon
sprouting an arrow—this way—$300 cab to Canada—
everyone trying—to figure out—how to get a plaque—
mother of the year—teacher of the year—*I got one last
year*—my passenger says—the engine running—I put
her walker—in the trunk—in honor of women—the
men cook—greasy hash browns—processed beef—with
a precision unknown—in human history—we can now
predict the life—of an engine part—78-year-old Ron Hill—
takes a rest—after running—every day for 52 years—and
39 days—we aim to grow old—gracefully—but an aim—is
only an aim—   *17 May 2017*

The Eye of the Observer

—heading East—on the Edsel Ford Freeway—Joni
Mitchell's *Blue*—the last time she saw Richard—was
Detroit in 68—soon Ford will create—energy-efficient
buildings—linked by self-driving vehicles—a snowy
night in 76—spinning around—on the ice—360 degree
turn—our baby on my lap—Allen driving—now I pass—
the giant Uniroyal tire—minutes later—exit Trumbull
Avenue—4711 Avery Street—back then—secretly—
dreaming—about a symphony musician—with a leather
shoulder bag—a good looking guy—shot heroin—my
brother says—he caught my eye and smiled—the
observer's eye—sometimes—pulls you into the center—at
28—I chose the periphery—Barbara Chover cut Allen's
hair—love so sweet—I let him cut mine—we sold our
motorcycles—and I started grad school—becoming—for
the time being—grownups with children—   *20 May 2017*

Me, Too

—rheumatic fever—turns the skin—yellow—a heart, scarred—soon—my mother says—you will—take my place—I wear her old stockings—dye my hair henna— like hers—smoke cigarettes—wear red lipstick—her fringed leather jacket—at 18—at the sewing machine— my foot is hers—pressing the pedal—there's a murmur— in your heart—the doctor says—but soon it will heal— in the afternoon—I birth a child—walk down the hallway—in her turquoise bathrobe—at the zoo—an old female orangutan—locks eyes—with a young woman— breastfeeding a baby—yes, she nods, *me, too*—at 37—my two children sound asleep—and all of a sudden—I wake up—surprised to be alive—what about—the others—I think—the motherless migrants—the refugees—the cumulative wound—rooms—that murmur—and whisper—remember me—take care of them—take care of you—   *20 May 2017*

The Only One

—in LA—a man on the street—sees a camera—makes a
u turn—starts posing—in NOLA—with Robert E. Lee—
removed—the police—take a break—at a walk-in beer
cooler—in Iran—couples now walk—hand-in-hand—the
Ayatollah blinks—his ever seeing eye—even though—the
bully tweets—anti-Muslim—this and that—the Saudis—
treat him—as royalty—they all sway—and dance—even
the bully's—top supporter—a billionaire financier—
who later—gets an enormous investment—from Saudi
Arabia—stroll along—on the east shore—of Lake
Michigan—my sister and I—buy a muffin—drive back—to
Kalamazoo—we watch—Jimmy Fallon—dancing with
Michelle—Stevie Wonder singing—after five months—
with the cruelty—ineptitude—Cloud Computing—breaks
away—rushes ahead—of Always Dreaming—and like
those in church—we sing along—our Michelle amour—
sweet as flowers—bloom in May—Michelle amour—the
only one that we adore—   *21 May 2017*

Pow!

—check into a motel—in Indiana—broken door—no
fridge—convey your trust—and sometimes—optimal
options—the Taliban overran—four security check
points—families on house lock down—lock out—at
dinner—my friend says—she voted—for a third party—
when we were girls—she could recite—every swear
word—in fifteen seconds—you helped—empower the
bully—unintended—albeit—now he's laying—his hate
hands—on our glowing orb—*just* politics—nothing more
to say—look at family photos—my father's car—and a
sign—vote for Nixon—vote for Vietnam—Mohammad Ali
said No No No—I won't go—Pow!—driving—I don't know
where—pitch dark—in a dirt parking lot—gps—map me
forward—miles across—the Atlantic—sixty ambulances—
speed toward carnage—in Manchester—hate begets
hate—so we strip—turn on the shower—Mr. Ali—the little
boy asks—can I have your autograph?—   *24 May 2017*

Tompkins Square

—on location—the Grateful Dead's—first East Coast
show—Prabhupada's first US kirtan—chanting and
dancing—a rebellious artifact—or ultimate destination—
to blow a trumpet—bang on some buckets—if I had
money—I'd buy a tiny apartment—across the street—a
comeback with millennials—a micro machine—
with its own heartbeat—trying to find a dot—in the
pacific—Amelia Earhart disappears—upward—an old
stately elm—leans toward me—then the voluminous
sound—of branches cracking—soon this tree will be
gone—in Mosul—Isis leaves behind—blurred Disney
figures—and piles of—religious rubble—gone like—the
birdhouse tree—men now say—they'll let women—
make birdhouses—to my left—a guy dozing—on a
park bench—a tropical print short-sleeved—button-
down—100 percent rayon—a lovely shade of blue—the
ultra rich have great views—but trees do poorly—in the
shade—I, on the other hand—love sitting here—under
the Krishna tree—eating chocolate—and looking—across
the street—at my old apartment—   *12 July 2017*

Ever-Shifting

—on the F—a woman scrolls, swipes—and eats—bits
of pastry—out of a brown bag—her round face—
surrounded—by shoulder-length—greasy hair—behind
me—a little boy to his friend—I'm scared of the
president—that's so sad—I say out loud—I'm not afraid—
the woman beside me says—I voted for *him*—do you regret
it now?—Nope—some Mexicans held up my friend—now
because of *him*—just because of *him*—352 Mexicans—have
been removed—from Staten Island—and I'm happy—
gone—swiped—away—mothers, fathers, children—some
get off—some get on—a young man—in a tee-shirt
and running shorts—stares into his cell—a man with a
black beard—gold-colored shawl—switches the screen—
hundreds of Muslim men bowing—over his shoulder—I try
to catch the name—of the Imam—over his shoulder—the
ever-shifting—wall between us—one after another—we
take the escalator—up and out—at Broadway-Lafayette—
scrolling through—our options—   *24 July 2017*

Room to Run

—dreaming downtown Detroit—an alley—a bomb
planted—don't tell anyone—instead—tap dance—on a
desk—in the First Federal Building—shuffling papers—
rearranging pens and pencils—ask the doctor—may
I leave—no, he says, no—minutes before—the first
explosion—running—past Kinsel's Drug Store—in one
door—down narrow aisles—out another—a home run—
past Greenfield's Cafeteria—when my economy—had
room to run—in Hudson's and Crowley's—the smell of
perfume—out the door—with scented keepsakes—so
alluring—they might cause—a shipwreck—past little
shops—on narrow streets—where high ladder fire trucks—
have trouble maneuvering—green high heels—and
matching skirt—catch the Jefferson Avenue bus—head
east—eighteen years old—in 67—looking out the back
window—St Jean burning—one building crumbling—after
another—Detroit implodes—behind me—my place, my
childhood—never to return—   *30 July 2017*

Fair Share

—in tick country—foxes in demand—first blood—to keep
down the mice—Mr. Fox tricks—the super bullies—for
a fair share—of the cider—stop by my ex's office—limp
in—say hello—*oh, my white girlfriend*—he laughs—happy
to see me—*when you text*—*my wife sees your photo*—delete
it—put up a fox—*I like seeing you*—his voice—like a
sensor—a measurement—of blood flow—and pressure—I
hurt my coccyx—I say—in yoga—his gift—a box of
needles—*can I come and see you?*—he asks—a needle
drags—across my chest—*have you been with anyone*—a pen
with several fine needles—creating tiny wounds—90%
wonderful—without insurance—a pair of needle-nosed
pliers—yanks out—an emotionally unavailable—rotting
tooth—at Stuyvesant square—Apple presents—a new
emoji—a fox in a headscarf—I trot down the hall—to
have blood drawn—by another doctor—he to a patient—
with his needles—   *3 Aug 2017*

Now and Again

—to cover misdeeds—puff yourself up—with exaggeration
and falsification—your allies—a glittering who's who—in
the corporate financial world—supporters—homegrown—
Detroit Right Wings—the eighth letter—their icon—88
HH for Heil Hitler—nonetheless—here we are—moving
along—as usual—on the train—an old woman—late
80s—her hands shaking—thin—wearing a baseball hat—
every human body—a marker in time—a squat woman—
body like a boxer—red dyed—ear length hair—unwinds
a long—snaking bracelet—carefully reorders—then
rewinds—glittering diamonds—on the 6 uptown—a skinny
guy—grey messy hair—tiny rimless glasses—tattered jeans
and shirt—reading a book—many paper markers—what is
it?—lean left—catch "Benjamin"—lean further—"lter"—
Walter Benjamin—every human body—a marker—to escape
Nazis—he took—an overdose of morphine—1940—at 51st
street—I stand up—have you read *Berlin Childhood?*—I
ask—*yes*—and he likes it too—my favorite Benjamin—did
you read the early version—the one—about the moon—*I
will*—he says—we nod—then off the train—walking
east—just as—the moon crosses over the sun—the city in
darkness—for a fleeting moment—   *21 Aug 2017*

Up, Over and Away

—the bully gives—bankers—free rein—with our
retirements—under the Manhattan Bridge—we climb
upward—clam shells—welded into the wall—the Q train
roars—overhead—give me a rock—give me a wall—the
bully has a tantrum—we scurry—for pennies—halfway
up, halfway down—halfway up—hoist a leg out this
way—the other—say *talaq*—three times—a man—gets an
instant divorce—Build a wall!—Lock her up!—the credit
calculated—roar and paw—the ground—ladies—here you
are—use anything—knife or stick—merely a fence—the
clam shells—uneven—our spines—do not like—uneven—
three times up—three times down—the next day—shape-
shifting—pavement cracked and uneven—fence him in—
a deserved comeuppance—the crowd roars—as the moon
passes—over the wall—over the sun—one limb lifting at a
time—we calculate—the distance—   *25 Aug 2017*

One Bridge Down

—down the corridor—standing—in the doorframe—in a
white coat—my ex—talking to a woman—a new sequel—
to wonder wife—behind the barrier wall—unnoticed—we
make a tunnel—press the button—on the elevator—
slip away—cut off—the winds kick up—powerful tidal
surges—one bridge down—everything south lost—finally
released—from a Syrian prison—the activist brushes—her
ten-year-old daughter's—long black hair—now strands
of white—adrift—we reconnect—with our feet—on
the floor—of the downtown train—unsteady—an aged
Chinese man—looks for a seat—look down—hide behind
a cell phone—you'll never be famous—on instagram—and
that's ok—emerge into daylight—some days—forgetting—
may be the only solution—   *12 Sept 2017*

Don't Worry

—twenty or twenty thousand—who can be sure—trees
or people—down the hallway—a whispered echo—I'll be
back—I'll be back—in a minute—I'll be back—slipping
into a forest of people—it's ok to drill—anywhere—says
the interior department—it's ok—stay right here—by
the door—I'll find her—the man says—slipping into
the crowd—outside—I watch—everything burning—
bereft—horrified—timber falling—weeping—in bed—I sit
up—cry out—my baby—behind me—a little boy—clears
his throat—now a serious narrator—don't worry—she
got away—out the back door—he goes on—and all the
animals escape, too—whew!—his brother nods—there it is
again—*that* voice—   *19 Sept 2017*

A Lot of Things

—a red and white striped shirt—goes round and round—
slipping back—then reappearing—first on a model—then
my daughter—then passed to me—my favorite—to
brighten—one's own path—Buddha said—one must
light—the path of others—in the filthy waters—after
Hurricane Harvey—a young man—repairs a house—an
accidental wound—a flesh eating bacteria—just like that—
nothing brings down—a leek—like a few grains—of sand—
or to wash—and wash and wash—sometimes—I look
into—the crowded drawer—of shirts—and think—oh, let
it rest—after the storm—the gorgeous wild—Puerto Rican
parrot—white-ringed eyes—a red stripe above its beak—
once millions—now less than 100—David Salle puts—a
lot of things—into his paintings—watermelon—a kleenex
box—we put a lot of things—into our apartments—but the
how—he says—is most important—in this case—the graffiti
artist uncaps—her black marker—and signs—the work of
art—accidentally—near the bottom seam—with a black ink
spot—and a tiny hole—   *1 Nov 2017*

In a Six Minute Stretch

—the Knicks lose the ball—ten times—the bully's hair—
blows up and out—in the wind—revealing—an empty
space—to the hidden director—cut, cut, cut—off to the
East Village—for a haircut—liven up a dull green salad—
with something distinctive—on 7th Street—my old super
Peter—hugs me—shakes his head—new people—come
and go—rents too high—thousands homeless in PR—two
hurricanes—and not on the GOP's list—of worthy ones—
to protect—bikers and pedestrians—from angry truck
drivers—new concrete barriers—how I miss—the ride—
across town—passing friends on the street—oh forget
it—the ever-shifting—everything—off to the store—for a
psong chair—like my ex had—can't have him—have the
chair—ha ha—you might want to consider—a hot tea—
or a jacket—with the wind—it could feel like 39—lean
back—in my new chair—working on a poem—then watch
a crime show—tragic loss—and the inevitable solution—
yellow leaves—on the ground—and the sun so bright—
it's almost blinding—   *3 Nov 2017*

Private Eye

—new lessons for cab drivers—in Karachi—don't look at a
woman—in your rear view mirror—don't say anything—
about her clothes—don't ask—if she's married—the exact
script—of rickshaw drivers—in Mysore—to a younger
me—now through a green tunnel—of trees on 12th
street—I walk to the car—turn on the radio—69 and my
eyesight a little blurry—what to do—an 18 year old girl—
testifies—the detective's partner watched—in the rear
view mirror—guilty of wearing—a nipple ring—then his
turn—keep your mouth shut—they said—in the women's
bathroom—my head hurts—coughing so hard—I could
burst—a brain vessel—Nick Buoniconti'll donate—his
brain—to science—they buy and sell—footballers—the
brains typically—come by fed ex—Dr. Vogel expects
Paddock's brain—any day—why did he—shoot—all
those people—Robert E Lee—says General Kelly—was
honorable—men and women—of good faith—*on both
sides*—even those—who owned and sold human lives—
as hedge funds—monetized—securitized—leveraged—
multiple times—then a good cotton and sugar season—in
1837—the banks collapsed—don't say a word—shut
your mouth—a tax cut—millions of dollars—for the most
privileged—I slam on the brakes—and just miss—a cyclist
swerving—into his cell phone—   *6 Nov 2017*

Leaf in Hand

—a linden tree—fills my window—with constant
movement—leaves falling—branches reaching upward—a
grasshopper—found—in the thick paint—of Van Gogh's—
Olive Trees—on the path—of Buddhist—compassion—
Rohingya village and trees—decimated—overnight—
puffball mushrooms—mysteriously pop up—underground
the roots branch—far and wide—like social networking—
intersecting—with white supremacist—and bully fans—
take a walk—up 7th Ave—to a street vender—purchase
a basket—made in Ghana—upwards—a towering
sycamore—underground—a network of old pipes—
extending—across the USA—a $300 billion dollar—war
to decide—who gets the contract—iron or plastic—up
the hill—and down the avenue—limping—with a broken
toe—past brownstones—old trees—bikes whizzing past—
a leaf in hand—a black ash—I think—   *11 Nov 2017*

Coyotes

—to give thanks—artists, film makers, writers—gather
here—some of the same—every year—no investment
capital—sloshing around here—perched on a stool—Bea
talks—about Al Franken—our comedian politico senator—
the sacrificial lamb—the real bully's—in the white
house—cackling—as we chant along—with Katie Lee—
Homo sapiens!—greedy pathetic fools—I'd rather be a coyote—
we quit drinking—Bea says—then we quit quitting—what
about Charlie Rose—and the women—who didn't look
elsewhere—a form of prostitution—for a media job—the
producers—infected—with variants of WannaCry—for a
minute or two—everyone in the room—is yelling—he's a
patriarchal pig—women are lucky—one guy says—they
can complain—when harassed—gay men can't speak up—
to clear our passageways and to let the creator hear our prayers—
Navajos run east—toward the first light—hollering—
and we head east—in the dark—on the F train—as it
wheezes—toward Brooklyn—   *25 Nov 2017*

Chocolate

—the dog whines—thumps her tail—pajamas—bare feet—
tiptoe down stairs—in the fridge—nothing sweet—no
left over pudding—scurry up—on the counter—quietly—
into the cupboard—a box of cooking chocolate—police
officers—lie in wait—nabbing—the child—who sneaks—
under the turnstile—unwrap a square—take a bite—
uck!—put it back—into the wrapper—into the box—who
took a bite?—who did it?—not me—not me—why so
skinny—second helpings—for the well fed—a lesson well
learned—early on—when they blow a whistle—we scurry
to our feet—slam into each other—enough—is enough—
why lavish a bully—with the acclaim—so clearly—he
demands—the forgotten white majority—where are we
going—our young lithe bodies—deep inside—these flesh
bags—heart throbbing—climb down—to get away—years
later—here alone—in the dark—*me, me, me*—throbbing—
oh so loudly—   *20 Feb 2018*

With a Bang

—with a bang—the hairy flower wild petunia—flings
its tiny seeds—sudden and far—how and why—the
scientist—kneels down—clamps a metal band—on
a pigeon's leg—her initials—and id number—my
broken toe—x-rayed, recorded—at the Bleecker Street
station—an old man—with head bowed—kneeling—on
cardboard—an over crowded—shopping cart, a sign—
repent—the end is near—the Indian guru whispers—the
only sin—to harm oneself—to harm another—is to harm
oneself—to repent too much—is to harm oneself—on the
platform—the next generation—leans over a keyboard—
riffs, breaks, runs—his body hunched—fingers flying—30
miles an hour—all at once—released—the seeds spin
outward—the bird flutters into the air—   *18 Mar 2018*

On the Carpet

—the boys and I—play—a board game—speculating—on
categories—*sickening?*—flip-flops, turtles, underpants or
the bully?—Logan goes crazy—with joy—*we know who—
we know who*—strikes over—~~America's promise—as
a nation—of immigrants~~—deliberately—stupid—
twitter—transparent—how could—a teacher—pull the
lever—for his education czar—I don't know—but we
know who—we know who—before the civil war—
senators shot—each other—over freedom—to own a
slave—then monuments—erected—in honor—of white
superiority—symbols linger—with—we know who—Luke
howls—hysterically—and then we dance—wildly—on the
carpet to—*I like turtles—they walk real slow—I like turtles—
they sit real low—* *25 Mar 2018*

Take a Cab

—to the food coop—the driver's skin—very dark and
leathery—deep wrinkles—in the rearview mirror—his
eyes drift downward—between the front and back—a
wide gap—clearly exhausted—hesitant—a hard struck
percussion—I stutter—*you-you been driving a cab long?*—
he clears his throat—sits up and speaks—a deep slow
resonant sound—*oh longer than I should—been driving
for via for a year—before that a car service—many years—
too many*—I cough—close the window—an increase in
pollution levels—*are you making less now—considerably and
working more*—a grandfather—I think—maybe a musician
or a singer—his voice echoes—deep in his lungs—and all
through the cab—the air we share—   15 *Apr 2018*

We Wait

—and wait—for the wild power of nature—*Om Nama
Shivaya*—anything—could happen—to turn around—
scream our lungs out—protesters in Gaza—under
the burning—midday sun—*Om Nama Shivaya*—gun
shots into the crowd—turn it off—turn it on—social
programs slashed—corporate greed—protections for the
environment—eliminated—the EPA rolls back—and
David Buckel—self-immolates—in the meadow—in the
park—*Om Nama Shivaya*—this winter—the coldest—since
1961—everyday when I hit—the sidewalk—I think—
it will never end—and yet—slowly and surely—the
temperature will rise—and the might and mystery—of
the cold wind—will surely spread—*Shiva—Brahma—
Narayana*—their seeds everywhere—*Shiva—Brahma—
Om Nama Narayanaya*— *24 Apr 2018*

Process Note

In 2016, I picked up a collection of writing and art by the dadaist, Elsa Von Freytag-Lorenhaven, also known as the Baroness.* I pored over this book, laughing at the way she took William Carlos Williams to task (old observations minted wisdom). She was the ultimate beat/punk artist, scoffing at bourgeois society. Reading her poems, I thought to myself—they are like ecliptic telegrams to the world. At the time I was collecting poetic material from my journals, arranging, rearranging and collaging in news from the days before and around. Meanwhile I felt desperate—as did many others—about the political situation unfolding in the country. Trump had not yet been elected, but the hate on mainstream media was shocking. Then he won the election—how horrifying. Greed, wealth, ignorance and hate arm-in-arm. While I'm nowhere near as anti-establishment or as abrasive as the Baroness, I did pick up on her rhythms and started translating my poems into ecliptic digital messages that I called "digigrams".

* *Body Sweats: The Uncensored Writings of Elsa Von Freytag-Loringhoven.* Edited by Irene Gammel and Suzanne Zelazo, MIT Press, 2011.

Acknowledgments

Thanks to the journalists in the *New York Times* for words, phrases and ideas collaged into these poems. And thanks to the editors who published these poems in their zines and magazines—Stacy Szymaszek, *The Recluse*; Ricky Ray, *Rascal*; Peter Bushyeager, *Keen*; Pete Spence, *Have Your Chill* and *Read On*; Jeff Wright, *Live Mag!*; Wren Tuatha, *Califragile*; Susan Lewis, *Posit*; John Tranter, *Journal of Poetics Research*; Ed Foster, *Talisman*; Anselm Berrigan, *Brooklyn Rail*; Michael Boughn, *Dispatches Poetry Wars*; Wayne Berninger, *Downtown Brooklyn*; Sanjay Agnihotri, *Local Knowledge*; Jamey Jones, *The Hurricane Review*; David Kirschenbaum, *Boog City Reader*; Peter Werby, *The Fifth Estate*; and Collin Schuster, *The Magnet*.

I am very thankful for all the support over the years from family and friends, especially Lewis Warsh. Thank you, Lewis for thirty-five years of friendship, our many lunches, dinners, letters, emails, phone calls, and for your continual support of my writing. Onward with love and peace.

Barbara Henning is the author of four novels and seven collections of poetry, most recently a novel, *Just Like That* (Spuyten Duyvil 2018); and poetry collections, A *Day Like Today* (Negative Capability Press 2015), *A Swift*  *Passage* (Quale Press 2013) and *Cities & Memory* (Chax Press 2010). Her current project is a hybrid documentary on her mother's life, *Look At Me—I Lived: Ferne, a Detroit Story (1921-1960)*. In the 90s, Henning was the editor and publisher of *Long News Magazine and Book*s; she is also the editor and author of *Prompt Book: Experiments for Writing Poetry and Fiction* (Spuyten Duyvil 2020). Born in Detroit, she presently lives in Brooklyn and teaches for Long Island University and writers.com

www.barbarahenning.com

UNITED ARTISTS BOOKS

unitedartistsbooks.com / spdbooks.org

114 W 16th Street, 5C, New York, NY 10011